Stand Up for Responsibility

Growing Character

By Frank Murphy

21st Century Junior Library

Published in the United States of America by
Cherry Lake Publishing
Ann Arbor, Michigan
www.cherrylakepublishing.com

Reading Adviser: Marla Conn, MS, Ed., Literacy specialist, Read-Ability, Inc.

Photo Credits: ©Rawpixel.com/Shutterstock, cover, 1; ©PedroMatos/Shutterstock, 4; ©TigerStock's/Shutterstock, 6; ©Maria Evseyeva/Shutterstock, 8; ©Deborah Kolb/Shutterstock, 10; ©Monkey Business Images/Shutterstock, 12; ©lovelyday12/Shutterstock, 14; ©Rawpixel.com/Shutterstock, 16; ©Svineyard/Shutterstock, 18; ©Rawpixel.com/Shutterstock, 20

Library of Congress Cataloging-in-Publication Data

Names: Murphy, Frank, 1966- author.
Title: Stand up for responsibility / written by Frank Murphy.
Description: Ann Arbor : Cherry Lake Publishing, 2019. | Series: Growing character | Includes bibliographical references and index.
Identifiers: LCCN 2019007380| ISBN 9781534147454 (hardcover) | ISBN 9781534148888 (pdf) | ISBN 9781534150317 (pbk.) | ISBN 9781534151741 (hosted ebook)
Subjects: LCSH: Responsibility–Juvenile literature.
Classification: LCC BJ1451.R24 M87 2019 | DDC 179/.9–dc23
LC record available at https://lccn.loc.gov/2019007380

Cherry Lake Publishing would like to acknowledge the work of The Partnership for 21st Century Skills. Please visit *www.p21.org* for more information.

Printed in the United States of America
Corporate Graphics

CONTENTS

Be responsible by getting your homework and chores done before playing.

What Is Responsibility?

Matthew called his friend Amir to ask if he wanted to come over and play a brand-new video game.

"Hey thanks, Matthew, but I can't tonight," said Amir. "I promised my mom I would help her wash the car."

"Aw man, that's cool! It's good that you're helping your mom," said Matthew.

Doing what you said you would do is being responsible.

Responsibility is doing what you are supposed to do, when you are supposed to do it, no matter how you feel. This means if you feel like playing a video game, but you are supposed to help someone do something, you should **honor** your **commitment**.

That's what Amir did. He would have loved to play that new video game. But he honored the commitment he made to his mom.

Having a good attitude while doing your chores is important.

Being Responsible

A responsible person is acting in a **mature** way. A mature person follows through with what they said they would do.

Since Amir told his mom he would help her, he kept his promise to her. On top of that, he showed maturity by not complaining about it. He followed through. He didn't complain. And he did a great job.

Being responsible also means making **wise** decisions. In other words, think before

Caring for a pet is a big responsibility.

you act or speak. Thinking about how your decisions will affect you and others is smart, mature, and responsible.

Your decisions could be as simple as looking both ways before you cross a street. If you don't do this, you're not being safe! It could be remembering to take your dog out in the morning. If no one is home during the day, it's not fair to your dog.

Create!

Ask a teacher or parent to help you create a poster with big block letters that spell the word *mature*, *wise*, or *responsible*. Then write in jobs you do and good decisions you make to show how you have been and will be responsible. Hang it somewhere to remind you how important it is to be responsible.

You are responsible for learning the information your teacher gives you.

At school, there are many ways to show responsibility. School is like your job. *You* are the one who is most responsible for your own learning—more than your parents, grandparents, or even your teacher. It's your job to listen, ask questions, and do the best work you can do! It's also your job to not make it difficult for other kids to learn. One way to do this is to follow school rules.

Ask Questions!

If you aren't sure about an assignment, ask questions. If you want to know more about a topic, ask questions. It's a teacher's job to help you find answers to your questions. Responsible kids ask questions.

Volunteering in your community is a great way to show responsibility.

Being Responsible in Your Community

Everyone—adults and kids—can help make the world a better place! Finding ways to **volunteer** is a great way to help, and it shows responsibility toward your community. Just like Amir volunteered to help his mom, you can ask your parents or teachers to help you find ways to volunteer in your neighborhood or community. It could be helping to raise money or doing a service project.

Everyone is responsible for taking care of our planet.

Another way to show responsibility is to care about our **environment**. Littering *does not* show responsibility. Throwing garbage in the proper containers *does* show responsibility. And **recycling** cans, bottles, and paper shows even more responsibility.

Think!

Think about things you see happening in the world that you wish you could change. It might be the litter that you see on the streets. It might be too many weeds in the yard of an older neighbor. It might be an animal shelter that has too many dogs and not enough workers. Volunteering is a great way to help solve the problems that are important to you.

It is irresponsible to leave things where they might get in other people's way.

No matter where you are, outside or inside, leaving a place better than you found it shows responsibility. It might be putting your bike in a proper and safe place, so it is not in anyone's way. It might be cleaning up your table and floor area in the school cafeteria, even if it isn't your mess. Maybe no one will notice that you cleaned up a mess that wasn't yours. But it's the responsible thing to do!

If you show responsibility, people will be able to trust and rely on you more.

The more you show responsibility, the more people know they can trust you. Your friends, family, and teachers will know they can count on you to honor your promises. Plus, you'll feel more mature.

Look!

Look for responsible people in your life. Maybe it's a teacher or a coach. What kind of choices do they make? Pay attention to your parents' efforts to make sure you have the things you need to be successful at school. They are showing you a way to be responsible for others.

GLOSSARY

commitment (kuh-MIT-muhnt) a promise to do something

environment (en-VYE-ruhn-muhnt) the world around you, including the land, sea, and air

honor (AH-nur) to do what you have promised to do

mature (muh-CHOOR) behaving in a responsible, adult-like way

recycling (ree-SYE-kuhl-ing) collecting used items that can be made into new products

volunteer (vah-luh-TEER) offer to do a job for no pay

wise (WIZE) having good sense or good judgment

FIND OUT MORE

BOOKS

Donahue, Jill L., and Mary Small. *Way to Be! How to Be Brave, Responsible, Honest, and an All-Around Great Kid*. Mankato, MN: Picture Window Books, 2011.

Suen, Anastasia. *Don't Forget! A Responsibility Story*. Edina, MN: Magic Wagon, 2009.

INDEX

ABOUT THE AUTHOR

Frank Murphy has written several books for young readers. They are about famous people, historical events, and leadership. He was born in California but now lives in Pennsylvania with his family. The most important thing that Frank is responsible for is his family.